THE DREAMWORK PAPERS:

THE DREAMWORK PAPERS:

AN INTRODUCTION TO THE PSYCHOLOGY OF DREAMS

Elizabeth L. Howard, M.A.

Edited By Grace Darcy, Carmel Valley, CA
and Beulah Trist, Carmel, CA

iUniverse, Inc.
New York Lincoln Shanghai

THE DREAMWORK PAPERS:
AN INTRODUCTION TO THE PSYCHOLOGY OF DREAMS

iUniverse books may be ordered through booksellers or by contacting:

iUniverse
2021 Pine Lake Road, Suite 100
Lincoln, NE 68512
www.iuniverse.com
1-800-Authors (1-800-288-4677)

ISBN-13: 978-0-595-37626-1
ISBN-10: 0-595-37626-6

Printed in the United States of America

LIST OF ILLUSTRATIONS

All credits and copyrights are listed within the body of the text.

INTRODUCTION

"Start at the beginning,
go on to the end, stop there."
Alice in Wonderland (1886)

I completed my B.A. degree in American Studies in 1978 and quickly went to work on what became an M.A. degree in Gestalt Therapy.

Vincent O'Connell, Ph.D., trained me in Gestalt Therapy, supervised my M.A. degree, and became my great and dear friend. I met Vincent in 1975 and, from then on, I kept a dream journal and became increasingly fascinated with dreams and dreaming.

I completed my M.A. thesis, "The Evolution of a Gestalt Therapist," in February of 1980 at Goddard College, Plainfield, Vermont, and received my Certification in Gestalt Therapy from Vincent O'Connell at the same time. I didn't write about Gestalt Therapy again until 1986, when I wrote a brief paper titled "Gestalt Therapy" for the *New Age Florida Journal.* Later, when I started doing dream workshops, I amended the article to include dreamwork. "Gestalt Therapy & Dreamwork," which follows this Introduction, was published in *Health Lights Journal* in 1988 and in *Elevations Journal* in 1989. That paper has again been amended to include more memories and details about gestalt therapy and dreamwork.

This book, *The Dreamwork Papers: An Introduction to The Psychology of Dreams*, is a collection of papers I have written over the years to introduce ideas about dreams and dreaming to all who are interested.

Some of these papers were published in newspapers, newsletters, and magazines, and some were handouts for lectures and classes. Some were written especially for this book. I offer here what I have learned and tell my own dreams and stories to share my love of dreams and their supportive and consoling power in my life.

Reference:

Carroll, Lewis, *Alice's Adventures Underground*, New York: Dover Pub. Inc., 1965 (A facsimile of the author's manuscript with additional material from the facsimile edition of 1886).

Chapter One

GESTALT THERAPY & DREAMWORK

"Gestalt Therapy is existential, experiential and experimental."
Laura Perls (1982)

Gestalt is a German word having to do with wholeness. Lore Perls, co-founder of gestalt therapy, says the word gestalt means "a philosophic, aesthetic concept" and involves processes, ongoing and ever-changing, which lead to the integration of personality (L. Perls, 1982.)

In formulating gestalt therapy, Frederick and Lore Perls drew upon a variety of traditions, such as psychoanalysis, Reichian character analysis, existential philosophy, gestalt psychology, and Eastern methods such as Zen Taoism. Also evident in the practice of gestalt therapy are Frederick Perls' desire to be a theater director and Lore Perls' early training in movement and dance.

The word gestalt is also used to indicate the situation at hand, here-and-now. Gestalt therapy very much deals with enabling a person to finish an old situation (close/finish/complete the gestalt) and move on to a new place where there is life and energy, i.e., ongoing gestalt formation.

For example, at the end of a love relationship, there is often much "unfinished business," such as undischarged anger and unspoken words. Likewise, in the case of a death, we frequently have more to say to the person who has died, whether in love or in anger or resentment. In these cases, there is a good-bye to be said, and then the moving on begins to happen. We are continually going through these processes, when we leave an old job, move to a new home, or say good-bye to some aspect of our present personality, perhaps some way of being that no longer works for us.

In gestalt practice, the approach can be very direct. If you are holding on to unexpressed feelings toward your mother, the therapist may ask you to face an empty chair with this suggestion: "Could you put your mother in the chair and say these things to her?" Thus, you will speak *to* your mother and not *about* her.

3

The emphasis here is on the dialogical approach and the I-Thou (rather than an impersonal I-It) relationship with the "self" and the "other" or the "other aspects of self."

The gestalt approach to understanding dreams is also very direct, for the dream is interpreted by the dreamer, not by the gestalt therapist. "What does your dream mean to you? What is your dream saying?" is the essential question here. For Lore and Frederick Perls, the developers of gestalt therapy, dreams were the "royal road to integration of personality," and they both worked extensively with dreams and dreamers.

In gestalt theory, everything in my dream is a part of myself. When I work in the gestalt way, I am the dream, I am the dreamer, I am the tree that appears in my dream, and I am the leaves and the earth and blades of grass. When I identify the tree and play the part of the tree, then I am the tree, and I am tall, green, and strong and I have roots. And so I say and learn, own up to and accept these things about myself—that I am an alive entity, a being-in-process, here-and-now.

The method in gestalt therapy is the dialogue. This dialogue can occur between the gestalt therapist and the dreamer, or the dreamer and the symbols of the dream. The therapist may ask the dreamer to "play the part of…" or "transform yourself into…" any dream symbol. Perhaps the dreamer might be asked to have a dialogue between symbols in the dream.

Two examples stand out in my memory. At a training workshop in Miami where Vincent O'Connell was the trainer and therapist, Vincent said to the dreamer, "What are your hands saying?" She did not answer. Then he said, "Create a dialogue between your hands." I do not remember the words of the dialogue she reported, but I can still see her hands vividly, "speaking to each other," in a discussion of the dilemma that was presented in her life.

Several years later, I was able to attend a workshop with Lore Perls at the San Francisco Gestalt Institute. Her clarity and compassion were inspiring. She worked with a woman who had dreamed of a horse. "Transform yourself into the horse," she said to the woman. The next thing I knew, the woman was "clip-clopping" around the room, and telling us what the "clip-clops" were saying to her.

Another method identified with gestalt is the use of the "hot seat" and the "empty chair." The dreamer may sit in a chair or on the floor, the dream symbols may be visualized on a pillow or on a chair, or the symbols may be represented by the actions of the dreamer. In any case, the person working on the dream (the dreamer) is on the "hot seat," and the chair or pillow or movements represent the "empty chair," where the dream symbol is placed. This brings "your mother," "the tree," or any dream symbol out of oneself, into the present moment, available for the dreamwork.

I wasn't able to meet Fritz Perls. He died in 1970, just before I began my gestalt studies. I was already fascinated with the gestalt approach when I met my teacher, Vincent O'Connell, and I was carrying one of the early books about gestalt therapy underneath the seat of my car when I went to our first meeting. Vincent was a friend, colleague and student of Fritz and Lore Perls in the "early days" in Columbus, Ohio. Fritz became much more famous during his time at the Esalen Institute in Big Sur, California, during the 1960's, and Lore is primarily known within the field of gestalt therapy, gestalt psychology and other psychotherapies. When Fritz was at Esalen he became somewhat confrontational and sometimes harsh, because he believed that some people did not want to "work" on their difficulties, but rather wanted to challenge him as a person and as a gestalt therapist. My knowledge of Fritz comes through Vincent, his memories of a softer and more compassionate Fritz, who spoke of gestalt therapy as "the sound of angels' wings."

Many "New Age" healers have adopted gestalt principles into music, dance, and occupational therapies. Gestalt therapy works toward healing those experiences of isolation, alienation, and desensitization that are so common in our culture today, for gestalt has to do with such contemporary issues as feminism, political and personal attitudes, considerations of how we may heal ourselves and our planet, and love.

Reference:

Perls, Laura, "A Conversation Between Laura Perls and Edward Rosenfeld," *VOICES: The Art and Science of Psychotherapy. Journal of the American Academy of Psychotherapists,* Summer, 1982.

Suggestions for Further Reading:

Fagen, J., and Shepherd, I.L., ed., *Life Techniques in Gestalt Therapy.* New York: Harper and Row, 1970.

Gaines, Jack, *Fritz Perls Here & Now.* CA: Celestial Arts, 1979.

Perls, F.S., Hefferline, R., and Goodman, P., *Gestalt Therapy: Excitement and Growth in the Human Personality.* New York: Dell Pub. Co., 1951. (Historical)

Perls, F.S., *Gestalt Therapy Verbatim*. Moab, Utah: Real People Press, 1969. (Fritz Perls' most readable book)

Polster, E., and Polster, M., *Gestalt Therapy Integrated*. New York: Random House, 1973.

Laura Perls.
Photo by Anje Reese. Used by
permission of *VOICES: The
Art & Science of Psychotherapy.*
V18, #2, '82. www.aapweb.com

Frederick S. "Fritz" Perls
At Esalen 1967.
Used by permission of
The Gestalt Journal Press.
www.gestaltjournalpress.com

Vincent O'Connell
My dear friend and teacher, at Little
Orange Lake, Hawthorne, Florida
Photo from the collection of
Elizabeth Howard, circa 1976.

Dreamer: Elizabeth Howard, 1987

Chapter Two

WOMEN DREAMING: A Workshop Using Gestalt Method

"Your shoes are too big,
A strange cat delivers a lecture
  on anthropology
Your teeth fall out,
You may be flying or falling…
What are you trying to tell yourself?
What is the answer here?"
Elizabeth Howard (1998)

"My shoes are too big." This is Erin's dream. She had taken over a job where she had "big shoes to fill."

"A strange cat delivers a lecture on anthropology." This is my dream, when I was working on my M.A. degree. The "cat" was anthropologist Claude Levi-Strauss. He was speaking in French, and in the dream I perfectly understood the language, and his complex theories.

The primary meaning of these two dreams was immediately evident to the dreamers, who felt that no further work was necessary. Sometimes, dreams are a puzzle and the answers to their riddles can help us along the path of our lives. That's why we have dream workshops, to figure out the mysteries and secrets of our dreams.

I started the Women Dreaming Workshop in 1987, in Florida. Since then, I've offered the workshop many times, in a great many different settings. As a feminist event, the workshop stands on its own…a gathering of women, sitting in a circle, a safe place to share dreams and life experiences. This is where we each learn to listen to and value our own voice and the voices of other women, speaking our truth.

These are the rules: No advice-giving. Only the dreamer may interpret the dream. If I make a suggestion about your dreamwork, please don't do it unless it feels right to you. My approach is gestalt therapy with its basic theory: Everything in a dream is a part of one's self. You may decide to put away, get rid of, any symbol of a fearful event or a person that you no longer want to have as a part of yourself and your life.

The most frequent dream is that of a house. Often, this is a recurring dream—an unfinished situation for an "unfinished woman." This kind of dream can be fun, and the dreamwork is often very fruitful in terms of self-knowledge.

Some variations of the theme begin with: "I'm a house. I'm large or I'm small, I'm young—or old—I'm green or white or blue or gold. I'm an attic, a basement, I'm shy or I'm bold."

Then I suggest: "Make a dialogue with the house. What does the house say to you? How do you respond? What does the attic say to the basement? How does the basement reply? Who's in the house? Is the house empty? What's behind that closet door? Will you nail the door shut? Will you look inside? Can you describe what you see? Will you play the part of the house, the attic, the basement, the emptiness, the fullness, the nails, the door, the hammer, the inside, the outside…Will you play the part of yourself, doing the work of the dream?"

Now make a statement about yourself. "Here and now I…Will you laugh or will you cry?" This is the dialogue, the work, which is the basic method of gestalt therapy.

Many dreams were told to me. Many times the impasse was breached. Many precious moments passed in the company of women, hearing each other's voices, learning to trust ourselves, to forgive, to know our boundaries, to say goodbye, to move on.

Each woman learned, again and again, that it is somehow more difficult to see the beauty in ourselves, "I'm a rose, I'm beautiful," than to see ourselves as the thorn, prickly and difficult. It is a great lesson to see our own goodness and appreciate ourselves.

I close this piece of writing by saying that I helped some women learn about themselves and to speak for themselves. This year, on International Women's Day 2003, I sat in a circle of 100 women and watched and listened as each woman spoke into the microphone. Some voices were shaking, and there were some tears, and we were speaking and listening as we each spoke of our dream of peace. I thought to myself, "I helped make this speaking possible." That's what can happen in dream workshops, when the teacher learns and the healer is healed. For this I give thanks and move on to the next experience of women dreaming.

Sharing our dreams and life experiences
Elizabeth Howard, 1986–87

Reference:

Howard, E., Workshop Flyer, 1998.

Chapter Three

SIGMUND FREUD:
In a Class by Himself

*"He was not only a genius but also, unlike many
geniuses, an extraordinarily nice man."*
Leonard Woolf (1967)

When we think of Sigmund Freud, the image evoked for many of us is of a bearded gentleman seated behind a couch smoking a cigar. We then recall that this is Dr. Freud, and the person who lies before him on the couch is his patient. These images are correct, but Freud was much more than a cigar, a beard, and a couch. His approach is called psychoanalysis, and he did ask his patients to lie quietly on a couch so that some of their resistances could relax and so that, while lying in a sleep-like position, they could better recall their dreams. Freud believed and taught that the interpretation of dreams is "the royal road into the realm of the unconscious." He encouraged his patients to say whatever came into their minds, using a free association of ideas.

Freud's best known book is *The Interpretation of Dreams* (1900). It is his most readable book and is virtually his autobiography. In its pages, Freud explains his theories and interprets his own dreams. He illustrates how a dream is the fulfillment of a wish, how dreams are based on events of the previous day, and he demonstrates the appearance of sexual symbols in dreams. In his preface to the 3rd Revised English Edition, Freud said of *The Interpretation of Dreams*, "It contains, even according to my present-day judgment, the most valuable of all discoveries it has been my good fortune to make. Insight such as this falls to one's lot once in a lifetime." (1931)

Freud's work has insured that we know about his ideas of different levels of consciousness: the conscious mind, which he said is the "tip of the iceberg;" below that the subconscious or pre-conscious mind, whose contents we can access but with some difficulty, and the unconscious mind, a huge repository of repressed and forgotten ideas, feelings and experiences, which can sometimes be accessed, perhaps in disguised form, in our dreams.

Freud's method of dreamwork is interpretative. The dreamer tells the dream and the therapist interprets. The surface content is called the "manifest" meaning of the dream, while the concealed meanings are called the "latent" content. A primary tenet of Freud's ideas centers around repressed sexual and aggressive feelings or wishes which, he said, frequently stem from childhood experiences and perceptions. According to Freud's symbology, a box would represent female genitalia and a cigar would be a male sexual symbol.

Freud shocked his colleagues and much of Victorian society with his ideas about sex and sexuality and his theories about childhood sexual impulses, i.e., the "Oedipus complex," which is the young boy's attraction to his mother and wish to kill his father; and the Electra complex in which the female in like manner is attracted to her father and wishes to rid herself of her mother. He opened the door to women's tales of sexual abuse in childhood and then slammed that door again when his colleagues scorned him. He wondered "what does a woman want?," and then decided it must be a penis, his famous theory of "penis envy."

Freud can be a very annoying person, with his ideas about women, and his sometimes rigid symbol interpretation of dreams. He was a man of his time and, in many ways, he did not attempt to move beyond his male dominated culture. Nevertheless, he really talked with and listened to his women patients, and he trained many women as psychoanalysts. Princess Marie Bonaparte, Lou Andreas Salome, and his daughter Anna Freud were all his students, and they were strong and fascinating women. He gave us a point of reference for much contemporary learning in psychotherapy, and his theories are worth our time to study. I sometimes find wishes in my dreams, and I can generally find the influence of the previous day. "Sexual symbols," when I discover them, are sometimes amusing, sometimes embarrassing, and they are a part of the dreamwork and the discoveries that I make about myself.

To write about Freud and his ideas in a few pages is a difficult task. Freud wrote many books and papers, and many books and papers have been written about him. He trained scores of students as psychoanalysts, and a number of those students went on to become well known in their own right. Carl Jung was his most famous student. Their parting was bitter and painful. Freud considered Jung to be his "crown prince," to be his successor in the kingdom of psychoanalysis. Jung had ideas of his own that included a more spiritual approach as well as his theories of the archetypes of human personality.

Otto Rank and Alfred Adler, who parted in order to pursue their own ideas and theories, were also students of Freud. Another of Freud's students, Karen Horney, is the person who refuted Freud's theory of "penis envy" and asserted that what women want is not a penis, but equal privilege and power to that of men. Freud's daughter, Anna Freud, did not dispute his theories, but rather went on as a psychoanalyst to study and write about our defenses to awareness. She was a compassionate person, who was also known for her extensive work with children who were injured and traumatized during World War II.

Freud, an atheist and a Jew, lived most of his life in his beloved Austria. In the late 1930's, when Hitler began to seize power in European countries, he ordered the burning of all psychoanalytic books and outlawed psychoanalysis in Germany. Hitler expelled all Jewish analysts and banned Jews from all scientific bodies. When the Nazis took over Austria in 1938, Freud clung to his home, but after his daughter Anna was detained for questioning by the Nazis, he finally consented to leave. His friend and student, Princess Marie Bonaparte, paid $4,824 to the Nazis to get him out of Vienna. His mouth cancer, which had persisted over a 20 year period, a result of his chain smoking cigars, became inoperable, and he died in London in 1939. Without him, we would not have counseling and psychotherapy as it exists today.

References:

Freud, Sigmund, *The Interpretation of Dreams*. (First published in 1900.) New York: Avon Books, 1965. The quotation on p.11 above appears at p.xxxii of the Avon Books edition of 1965 and is attributed to Freud in Vienna, March 15, 1931.

Woolf, Leonard, *Downhill All The Way: An Autobiography Of The Years 1919 to 1931*. New York: Harcourt, Brace & World, Inc., 1967.

Website, Freud Museum London. www.freud.org.uk/

Suggestion for Future Reading:

Freeman, Lucy, *Freud and Women*. New York: Ungar, 1981.

Sigmund Freud. He was much more than a cigar,
a beard and a couch.

Chapter Four

FIRST TO SLEEP AND THEN TO DREAM

There are several sleep disorders, such as narcolepsy—a rare sleep disorder where the person suddenly falls asleep during ordinary waking activities—and sleep apnea, which is characterized by sudden interruption of breathing during sleep. We are all familiar with insomnia, in which the person sleeps less than desired. Many of us have experienced some degree of insomnia. There are "long sleepers" and "short sleepers," and there are those of us who remember many dreams and those who remember a few. One thing is for certain—in order to dream, we must sleep.

It has generally been the function of researchers in university "sleep labs" and elsewhere to study sleep disorders. Sleep laboratories generally do not concern themselves with the meaning of dreams, but only with the physiological functions and stages of sleep itself. Monitoring is accomplished by attaching an electroencephalogram (EEG) and other brain or biological monitoring apparatus to the subject, who then sleeps in a bedroom-like room within the sleep laboratory facility.

The connection of REM, or "rapid eye movement" sleep to the dreaming state was discovered in 1953 when Eugene Azerinsky, an assistant in the laboratory of Dr. Nathaniel Kleitman at the University of Chicago, noticed a correlation between movements of the eyes beneath the eyelids of the sleeper and certain patterns of brain wave activity on an EEG. Since then, countless people have been connected to an EEG and other monitors in sleep laboratories and then awakened and questioned in order to match brain waves with depth of sleep, as well as to dream or dreamless sleep reported. Researchers have learned that a high proportion of sleepers, when awakened in the REM state, report they are dreaming. Even people who go into the sleep lab situation attesting they "never dream" will report a dream when awakened during the REM stage.

As we first drift off to sleep, we go through a stage that is called the hypnagogic state. It is then that we may experience "myclonias," a falling sensation or "jumpy legs." While in the hypnagogic state we may even experience vivid visual or auditory sensations that have a hallucinatory feeling. These vivid sensations sometimes jerk us back into wakefulness.

If you want to experience the hypnagogic state, you can experiment in the following fashion. Use a repeat alarm clock that rings every five minutes. If you are sufficiently awake, you can depress the stop bar every five minutes, and the alarm will not sound. If you are awakened by the alarm, you are likely to be in the hypnagogic state and can record its content. Another alerting technique is to hold a book or spoon in one hand while balancing the arm vertically, elbow on the bed. As you pass into the twilight state, the arm will fall and the object will drop, startling you back to consciousness. (Meyers, 1993)

As the night goes on, we pass from lighter to deeper sleep and then back again, moving back and forth throughout the night. We experience about five REM or dreaming periods, with the last or closest one to waking being the longest and most likely to be remembered. If you ordinarily go to sleep around 11 p.m. and sleep through the night and want to wake during a dream, first try setting an alarm for 4 a.m. to see if you are dreaming. You can even go so far as to set an alarm clock to wake you every two hours during the night, and you will almost surely catch a REM state and a dream at some point.

The study of sleep and dreams is part of the study of consciousness, from wide awake awareness, to "daydreaming," to the sensation of "falling" off to sleep, to full dreaming or REM sleep. Beyond the physiological need for sleep, many people find their dreams interesting, and some of us find them meaningful, consoling, and even inspiring.

Reference:

The primary source for the information on sleep and sleep labs is the David Meyers textbook, *Exploring Psychology.* New York: Worth Publishing Co., 1993.

Chapter Five

INSPIRATION, PROBLEM SOLVING AND DISCOVERIES IN DREAMS

"Learn to dream, gentlemen."
F.A. Kekule, the German chemist, at a scientific convention in 1890

Important discoveries have been made in dreams. For example, Robert Louis Stevenson dreamed the plot of *Dr. Jekyll & Mr. Hyde*, Frederick August Kekule found the secret of the structure of the benzene molecule in a dream, and Otto Loeur "dreamed up" his experiment demonstrating the chemical mediation of nerve impulses for which he won a Nobel Price for Physiology in 1938. Elias Howe invented the sewing machine as a result of a dream; William Blake and Paul Klee received inspiration for their art work; and Mozart, Beethoven, Wagner, Tartini and others dreamed of their musical compositions. Ingmar Bergman dreamed ideas for his work with films and Judith Guest dreamed screenplays. As if that weren't enough, Jack Nicklaus made a discovery in a dream that improved his golf game by 10 strokes.

Edgar Cayce, who was called the Sleeping Prophet, improved his grades in school as a child by sleeping on his school books. When he awakened he knew his lessons and went from being a below average student to an exceptional one. In adulthood, he was able to give extremely accurate information regarding health problems and other issues to people who consulted him, by receiving information during a dreaming or sleep-like state.

Many prophetic and inspirational dreams of religious origin have been recorded. It is part of Christian beliefs that an angel came to Mary, the mother of Jesus, in a dream to tell her that she would be the mother of a savior. The birth of the Buddha was also foretold to his mother in a dream. The "call to prayer" of the Islam tradition was described to Abdallah ben Zayd in a dream. These dreams have a spirituality that is religious and inspirational, going beyond the personal and possessing a quality of endurance, with directions that so influenced the dreamer that we still know about these dreams today.

Reference:

DeBecker, Raymond, *The Understanding of Dreams And Their Influence on the History of Man*. New York: Bell Publishing Co., 1968

Chapter Six

HOW TO REMEMBER YOUR DREAMS

"Listen, said the voice.
This is your dream.
I'm only stopping here for a little while.
Don't be afraid."
Mary Oliver, "Banyan"(1986)

The most important thing about remembering dreams is that you must really want to remember them. Dreams are about the wisdom inside ourselves, as well as unprocessed information, hopes, fears and wishes. In many traditions, dreams are regarded as messages to be spoken of and explored with others.

A good example of a dream-valuing culture was reported by anthropologist Kilton Stewart. Stewart traveled to the Malay Peninsula in 1935 where he studied the lives and dream practices of the Senoi people. At the time of his research, the Senoi had not reported a violent crime for two or three hundred years. They had a democratic culture, with all decisions made by consensus. Both adults and children reported little emotional disturbance or physical illness. Stewart lived with the Senoi for a year, and then experimented with their practices for fifteen years. (Stewart, 1935)

According to Stewart, the Senoi shared their dreams in a group every morning. Children were taught from an early age that dreams are for learning and for sharing. If a child had a frightening dream—say about falling—then he or she would be encouraged to "fall to the source of your power." Each child was encouraged to relax and enjoy such dreams and to learn from these dreams about the personal power of the individual. A song or story from a dream would be shared with the group and, if a child dreamed of a new device for cooking, for example, then the child would be encouraged to try it out, whether or not it seemed practical. The Senoi, said Stewart, believed that dreams are real. Therefore, if someone dreamed that he or she had injured a friend, an apology to the friend would be in order.

Stewart attributed at least a portion of the high mental and emotional functioning of this group to their use of dreams for personal growth as well as a source of knowledge.

Stewart's work has stirred controversy within the dream community, primarily because later researchers could not locate the specific dream practices or elicit similar information from informants. The controversy has now made its way to the Internet, and if you are interested, a good place to start is with Stewart's own 1935 article, which is published on www.dr-dream.com/kilton.htm.

If you want to remember your dreams, then read books about dreams, listen to music about dreams, watch videos about dreams, or attend a class on dreamwork. These experiences intensify the faculty of remembering dreams as well as expanding our understanding of ourselves.

METHODS:

- Before you go to sleep, tell yourself that you want to remember your dream, that you will wake up after your dream, and that you will remember your dream.

- Keep a notebook and pen by your bed, where you can reach them easily. You could also use a tape recorder. Be sure you can reach the light switch or place a flashlight by your notebook or tape recorder.

- We have several dream periods nightly. You can sometimes catch a dream by setting an alarm to wake you every two hours, or by waking earlier and more quickly than usual.

- Within the realm of "scarey" and troubling dreams are anxiety dreams; there are also nightmares, which are frequently based on the present life of the dreamer, and there are post-traumatic nightmares which are based on life experiences in the past. The nightmare will lose some of its power to frighten you when you have worked to understand its message. I once had a student in a dream class, a young man who was horribly abused in his childhood. Since that time all of his dreams were nightmares resulting from the terrible physical and emotional trauma he had suffered. Hearing other students talk of happy positive dreams was helpful, as was his sharing some of his frightening experiences. Before the end of the semester, he had a peaceful, non-frightening dream. Quite an accomplishment! This is an example of a post-traumatic, repetitive dream of emotional injury. Anxiety dreams generally come during lighter stages of sleep and reflect worries from the preceding day or dread of the day to come. Once we identify this type of dream, we can begin to work out actions and solutions to the problems that follow us into our dreams.

- Lucid dreaming is reported by some dreamers as an antidote to nightmares and anxiety dreams. In lucid dreaming, we learn to know we are dreaming, while in the dream state. Carlos Castaneda reported a type of lucid dreaming that was urged upon him by his teacher, Don Juan, who told him to "see your hands" in his dreams. Stephen LeBerge, Ph.D., of Stanford University, working in a contemporary setting, connected dreamers to an EEG, watched for the REM state, then flashed a light. When the dreaming person perceives the light flashing, he or she can learn to become aware of "now I am dreaming." Then the person can turn to face the monster or fly away from the crashing vehicle, for example.

- Even dreams of death, which can be the most frightening of all, often symbolize the "dying" of a part of the personality or even the end of a project. Dreaming of one's own death can be terrifying, but it is then that we can think quietly about the changes happening in our lives, the endings and new beginnings that happen on a daily basis. The dream of the death of a child or a dear friend can certainly be worrisome and sad, but most of these dreams are not predictive, but rather a sign that we can think about the changes and the ebb and flow of that relationship. Freud once interpreted a woman's dream of the death of a friend as her wish to see a gentleman she admired, who she knew would attend such a funeral!

- When you awaken from a dream, lie quietly: keep your eyes closed and remember the dream. Then, sit up and write down the dream in as much detail as you can remember. Where you are in the dream…what the colors are…who the other characters are…what you hear…what your emotions are…what the "action" is…and what your feelings are when you awaken from the dream.

- You can use a dream pillow or a dream catcher to symbolize and assist your desire to be in touch with your dreams.

References:

O'Connell, A. and O'Connell, V., *Choice & Change: The Psychology of Holistic Growth, Adjustment & Creativity.* New York: Prentice Hall, 1974. This is a classic textbook that has been published in several editions. It is the primary source here for suggestions on remembering your dreams.

Oliver, Mary, *Dream Work*, "Banyan." Boston: The Atlantic Monthly Press, 1986

Suggestions for Future Reading:

Castaneda, Carlos, *Journey to Ixtlan: The Lessons of Don Juan.* New York: Simon & Schuster, 1972.

LaBerge, Stephen, *Lucid Dreaming.* New York: Ballantine Books, 1985.

Stewart, Kilton, "Dream Theory in Malaya" © 1935. At www.dr-dream.com/kilton.htm

Chapter Seven

HERBAL DREAM PILLOWS

Herbal dream pillows are fun to make. A 3 x 4 inch piece of fabric is large enough, made from pretty scraps of material and stuffed full of lovely dried herbs. Just as people have personalities, herbs have "personalities" that are called properties. Relaxation and stimulation are physical properties of some herbs, while development of intuition is a metaphysical or emotional property. When selecting herbs for pillows, use your intuition. If you don't care for the scent or feel of a particular herb, then there will be another with similar properties. For example, chamomile is well known as a relaxing herb but some people don't care for its scent. You could substitute red clover, which has very little scent but is relaxing as well. The herbs I describe here are readily available and inexpensive. You can make a larger pillow by using buckwheat hulls or flax seeds as fillers with the herbs.

Chamomile: Chamomile is well known as an herb for relaxation. It has a rather distinctive scent, and the rhyme to go with it is: "First to sleep and then to dream, with lovely, soothing chamomile."

Rosemary: Rosemary is for remembrance. Keep a little pillow stuffed with rosemary by your bed, and it will help you remember your dreams. Used in herbal oils, rosemary is a bit stimulating—therefore, it stimulates dream recall, but it will not keep you awake.

Lavender: Lavender has a lovely color and scent. It is somewhat relaxing. Lavender will bring sweet dreams of fairies and pleasant scenes and will also help you develop more intuition.

Rosemary for remembrance

Chapter Eight

THE MAGIC COOKIE

I first heard about "The Magic Cookie" from Dr. Gary Pellettier, University of Nevada at Reno, when he came to my Psychology of Dreams class to give a talk. Students had a lot of fun experimenting with the "magic cookie." You can try it for yourself and see what happens.

> Before you go to bed at night eat one half of a cookie.
> Tell yourself that you will dream and that when you wake
> up in the morning you will remember the dream.
> Go to sleep. Dream. Wake up. Eat the other half
> of the cookie and you will remember the dream.

This worked for more than half of the people in my classes who tried it. It's O.K. to brush or floss your teeth after eating the half cookie before you sleep.

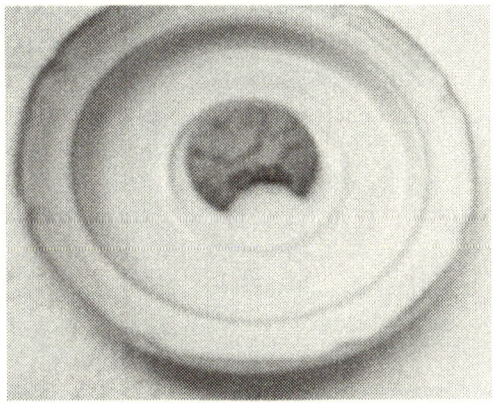

The Magic Cookie

Chapter Nine

PREPARING A DREAM JOURNAL

For recording your dreams, select a special notebook and pen to keep near your bed, with a lamp or light for use during the night. Record your dreams as soon as possible after awakening. You may want to purchase or make such items as dream catchers or dream pillows to focus your attention and express your invitation and welcome to the dream. When recording your dreams, date your dream and specify when you remembered the dream—whether you recorded it during the night, in the morning, or later in the day.

Write in the present tense, i.e., "I *am* walking down the street, when I *see...,*" instead of (past tense), "I *was* walking down the street, when I *saw...*"

This seems like a simple instruction; however it takes some time, attention, and determination to stay in the here-and-now, to bring your dream to the present moment.

After you write your dream, devote a sentence or two to your feelings about the meaning of the dream and how it relates to your life. You may want to give your dream a title, for example, "Walking Down The Street."

Note the approach you take to interpreting the dream, e.g., does it fit with a certain psychological theory? Do the colors or numbers have special meanings for you? Can you learn more by creating a dialogue with dream characters and symbols? Do you feel like illustrating the dream by drawing a picture? Some dreams are "big dreams," and you may have to spend more time writing, illustrating, even listing the dreamwork and dialogues that follow.

I've been keeping dream journals for about 30 years now. I have them all in notebooks and folders. My dreams have foretold my future many times. Reading back into my dreams spurs "remembrance of things past," introspection, smiles and tears...valuing of my life and the lives of others who have touched me along the way.

Value your dreams and record their messages in your journal. Find time and space in your life to savor your daydreams, night dreams and hopes-and-dreams. Your dreams will respond to your interest.

Dream Journals

Chapter Ten

DREAMS & THE STRESS OF LIFE

"Keep as cool as you can.
Face piles of trials with smiles.
It riles them to believe
That we perceive
The web they weave
And keep on
Thinking free"
The Moody Blues (1970)

Spring 1998. I'm very new to Monterey. As I write, I sit waiting for the tow truck and driver to come and help me start my pickup truck, which has dumped me outside a local office complex. I've been trying for days to write this paper, and I realize I've already dreamed about today. In my dream, my granddaughter and I are escaping from the Nazis. There are motor vehicles and train transfers and money changing, confusion and fear.

When I begin to work on my dream, I recognize the immediate past. I had just left Nevada, leaving behind or escaping from a part of myself that had become rigid, angry, and Nazi-like. My granddaughter made the trip with me. She represents the youthful, innocent part of me. I'm rescuing her, getting her away before it's too late, before her beauty and innocence are crushed beneath the Nazi boots.

Here-and-now, in this present day, I've made it to Monterey, to the ocean. The sun is shining, and I know and feel and sense that, like my truck, I need repair and nurturance so I don't crack under the strain that prevailed in my life over the last year.

Each dream has a special meaning for the dreamer. Since I've been in Monterey, many people told me that, after El Nino, which brought torrential rains and flooding, they dream often of water, rain, and the ocean. One woman

28

dreams over and over of the tree that fell in her yard, blocking her doorway and barely missing her home. If she had been at home when the tree fell, she would have been trapped inside. A natural disaster such as a flood or tornado threatens our homes, our livelihood, and even the lives of our families and ourselves. Loss and threat of loss create stress, and continued stress can break down the immune system, leaving us vulnerable to physical or emotional illness. The repetitive dream of trauma is one of the distinguishing symptoms of Post Traumatic Stress Disorder, which begins with the experience of an unusual and frightening circumstance. It is this type of reaction that is felt now by many residents of the Monterey Peninsula after the severe and unusual weather of the El Nino.

To facilitate healing from a traumatic experience, it is well to acknowledge the trauma and plan for extra rest and relaxation. This is a good time to remember our resolutions to eat well and to maintain schedules of physical exercise. You may want to sign up for a class, get a massage, read a new novel or just luxuriate in a bubble bath. Ask your dreams to come to you to speed your healing. As healing begins, dreams may reflect the process of rebirth, and such symbols as babies, young children, buds and blooming plants may appear.

Water itself, while frightening in the post traumatic state, has a traditional association with the unconscious mind, birth, rebirth and cleansing. While resting, we may take the opportunity to reflect on the symbols that have a personal meaning of new beginnings and how we wish to proceed again along our path.

El Nino welcomed me to the Monterey Peninsula and, in the midst of the storms, I experienced a warmth and a welcome. As I wait for the tow truck to arrive, I feel the sun on my back, and I smile and invite the next dream to come, with healing.

Reference:

The Moody Blues. Deram Records. Album: "In The Beginning." Song: "On The Threshold of a Dream." Circa 1970.

Chapter Eleven

DREAMS & THE PROJECTION OF ANGER

"First you look through a window,
and suddenly you recognize that you are just looking into a mirror."
Frederick S. Perls (1969)

We will deal here with one aspect of anger—the projection of one's own anger onto another person or group—and how we can "own" the projection through dreamwork.

We learn and introject our anger from our parents; we develop our own personal angers, and we sometimes develop righteous angers at other people and "the system." We may perceive anger as negative, unattractive and dangerous and, therefore, through the unconscious mechanism of denial, prevent ourselves from knowing we are angry. Since we cannot repress the anger entirely, and we do not wish to see ourselves as angry people, we then project our anger onto others (sometimes called "dumping" or "scapegoating.") For example, I am angry. I don't want to know or accept that I am angry. I project my anger onto my neighbor, and I suddenly see my neighbor as an angry person. Sometimes, a whole group of people may become scapegoats for our own unacknowledged anger, as when we project upon blacks, whites, native Americans or any group we perceive as different from ourselves.

The dream is an excellent place to look for anger projection. I recently dreamed my daughter was very angry with me. When I begin to work on the dream and take responsibility for the dream, I quickly learn I am angry, a bit, at myself for various failings I perceive in my "self." At that point, the anger is "out," I can forgive myself. and I can see more clearly how to proceed with my life.

In these times, it seems I wake up each day to some new cataclysm: schoolyard shootings, terrorist bombings, and always a war somewhere. To reclaim the misdirected energy of our anger and rage, to consciously direct that energy to the integration of the self and to the achievement of one's highest potential, would be to move decisively toward the dream of peace.

Reference:

Perls, Frederick S., *Gestalt Therapy Verbatim.* Moab, Utah: Real People Press, 1969.

Chapter Twelve

DREAMS, HEALTH & THE MIND-BODY CONNECTION

"I just wanna have a little fun before I die".
Sheryl Crow (1993)

The dreamwork process is traditional in healing mind, body, and spirit. In the 5th Century B.C., in ancient Greece, worshippers of Asklepios, the God of healing and medicine, traveled to his Dream Temples, where they slept, asking for a dream that would diagnose, give a remedy, or even heal their ailments.

Sleep itself is a great healer, and, as Shakespeare said, "knits the raveled sleeve of care." Refreshed and renewed, we deal better with the pressures and stresses of our everyday lives.

With dreamwork, emotional healing usually becomes visible first, sometimes through tears, sometimes with laughter or a great rush of anger. Later, we see that a healing on the emotional level opens us to healing on the physical and mental levels as well.

Patricia Garfield, a clinical psychologist and contemporary dream therapist, wrote about her experience with a misdiagnosed injury to her wrist. She was in terrible pain and in danger of permanent damage, until she listened closely to her dream messages and sought another medical approach. In her book, *The Healing Power of Dreams* (1992), she describes her experience and the experiences of her clients who used dreams for healing.

Each dream is unique to the dreamer and has its own special meaning and message. When I work with dreams, I use a dialogue method that allows the person to actively work with her or his dream characters and symbols. The following excerpt from my dream journal illustrates dreamwork using dialogue with the egg of my dream, a day of self-healing, a rhyme, and a smile to help me heal my life.

A Dream and a Day of Self Healing

"I woke in the night from a dream of an egg. I told myself to remember the dream and savor enlightenment yet to come. Early in the morning, I began to work on the dream.

The Dreamwork:

I'm an egg, I'm fragile, I could crack

I'm an egg, still safe in the womb of my mother.

I'm the egg of a chicken, a bird, or a snake.

I'm an egg hardboiled, fried, scrambled and eaten!

I've had a lovely day, full of sunshine, puttering around the house, napping with my kitty, contemplating my fragility, feeling a very real "fear of the market place." I've indulged myself with baths, food, and fantasies of a Mexican getaway. I allowed myself to rest, without giving myself a hard time. Now it is evening, and I've watched the lovely sky from pink dawn to brick red sunset. I drink more water, start a pan of rice and give thanks for a day of love and self healing."

This time I listened carefully to the wisdom of the dream. I didn't want to crack or get cooked and eaten, so I simply took a day off for rest and contemplation. The therapy was effective and I was able to go on with my work and my life.

Natural healers know that there is a mind-body connection and that, when we begin to heal one aspect of ourselves, our whole being is affected and can begin to heal also. Allopathic or "M.D." medicine reached a position of great power in the early 1900s, and the practice of medicine began to move far away from the "whole person" and rather saw the disease, the organ, or the cell rather than a person in need of healing. More traditional methods of healing, such as homeopathy and herbalism, were disdained by the majority of medical doctors.

As time has gone on, we now see a resurgence of the need to take control of our own health—to address the mind, body, spirit, and emotions—and to seek out healers who can see each of us as a whole person. As thinking individuals, we have begun to learn again to understand the "power of positive thinking" and to use gentle remedies that we can find for ourselves. Herbal remedies have become popular again, and homeopathic and naturopathic physicians are more in evidence. Oriental medical approaches such as Chinese herbal medicine, acupuncture, and Reiki—the Oriental method that uses symbols and transmission of energy to unblock the flow of "chi" or energy—as well as flower remedies, such as those first formulated by Dr. Edward Bach, that begin to gently heal emotional states. There also is crystal healing, which uses quartz crystals and other stones as energy amplifiers and healers. All these healing arts have again gained respectability. Biofeedback practitioners have formed a bridge that demonstrates how the mind can influence physical responses. Sensitive medical doctors have begun to listen to the needs of the whole person. Carl Simonton, M.D., and Stephanie Mathews-Simonton were using healing visualizations with their patients as early as the 1970's. Dean Ornish, M.D. uses meditation and visualization in his work with heart attack patients, and Bernie Siegel, M.D., includes the study of dream messages in his work with cancer patients.

Both now and in times past people have experienced physical injury and disease as well as the emotional states of fear, anxiety and depression. With all the information that we have before us today we can learn to heal ourselves and to find helpful healers when we need them. It is now more important than ever that we include our dreams as a part of our growth, maintenance, and healing of body, mind and spirit.

References.

Cooper, W., Crow, S., Bottrell, B., Baerwald, D., Gilbert, K., Album "Tuesday Night Music Club," Song "All I Wanna Do", WB Music Corp. etc., 1993.

Garfield, P., *The Healing Power of Dreams*. New York: Simon & Schuster, 1991

Suggestions for Future Reading:

Bach, Edward and Wheeler, F.J., *The Bach Flower Remedies*. New Canaan. Conn.: Keats Publishing, Inc., 1997.

Kent, James Tyler, M.D., *Lectures on Homeopathic Philosophy*, Richmond, Ca.: North Atlantic Books, 1979

Kloss, Jethro, *Back to Eden*. Santa Barbara, Ca.: Woodbridge Press Publishing Co., 1975. "Classic guide to herbal medicine, natural foods and home remedies." First published by Jethro Kloss in 1939.

Moyers, Bill, *Healing and the Mind*. New York: Doubleday, 1993

Ornish, Dean, M.D., *Dr. Dean Ornish's Program for Reversing Heart Disease: The Only System Scientifically Proven to Reverse Heart Disease Without Drugs or Surgery.* N.Y.: Random House, 1990.

Raphael, Katrina, *Crystal Enlightenment*, V. I, New York: Aurora Press, 1985

Siegel, Bernie S., M.D., *Peace, Love & Healing: Bodymind Communication & the Path to Self-Healing: An Exploration.* N.Y.: Harper Collins, 1991.

Simonton, O. Carl, M.D., and Simonton, Stephanie Matthews, *Getting Well Again.* Los Angeles, Ca.: J.P. Tarcher, 1978.

Stein, Diane, *The Essential Reiki*, Freedom, Ca.: The Crossing Press, Inc. 1995

Wise, Anna, *The High Performance Mind: Mastering Brainwaves for Insight, Healing & Creativity*, Los Angeles: J.P. Tarcher. 1997

Chapter Thirteen

ANN FARADAY &
DREAM POWER

*"...The cardinal rule in all cases being never
to impose a meaning on a dream but to allow it at all times
to 'speak for itself.'"*
Ann Faraday, 1972

Ann Faraday first published *Dream Power* in 1972. Thus, her work is completely contemporary in nature. Faraday conducted her own sleep laboratory experiments and studied the work of Freud, Jung, Perls and others. Her analysis of these important psychological theorists is easily readable. At times, Faraday uses her own dreams to illustrate these methods. Her explanations are so well presented that I used her book as a textbook for a course called *The Psychology of Dreams* that I taught at Truckee Meadows Community College in Reno, Nevada for several years.

Faraday also introduces Calvin Hall, an important teacher in her own studies. Hall's dream research is called "content analysis" and focuses on the dreams of "normal" (rather than troubled or "mentally ill") people. Hall collected over 10,000 dreams during the 1940's and, in 1953, he published *The Meaning of Dreams,* in which he published his findings. According to Faraday, Hall, differing from Freud, found that dreams did not disguise their true meaning with symbols. Hall used a kind of association process to assist dream interpretation and believed that any "clear thinking" person could probably understand her or his own dreams.

Faraday says her own interest is in the individual and personal meaning of each dream. She sees what she calls the "Three Faces of Dreaming": (1) Looking Outward: The things we may have failed to notice in waking life; (2) Mirrors: Reflections of our attitudes and prejudices; (3) Looking Inward: Giving existential messages about the state of our inner world. This aspect of dreams can reveal the hidden source of problems and help us to regain long buried aspects of personality.

Faraday believes in a comprehensive approach to the study of dreams and dreaming. Her approach and method is eclectic, using what is of most value to us in each approach, with emphasis on the theories and methods of Hall and Perls, and using Jung as a background influence. She does not discount the importance of Freudian psychoanalysis, and believes that, although many of our dreams can be interpreted on a practical "self-help" basis, the assistance of a counselor or psychotherapist, and the influence of a supportive group can be of great importance in times of need. She continues to recount her own dreams, as well as the dreams of her friends and clients, explaining how she and others came to their own interpretation of the dream.

Faraday begins to wrap up the book with a chapter she calls "Looking Forward: Dream Power in Society." She then predicts what has actually happened in the last 30 years: "…a mushroom growth of therapeutic and educational groups of all kinds in which ordinary people come together for the express purpose of promoting self-knowledge and personal growth." She goes on to suggest ways that we might be able to use dream power in our families, our churches, our educational system, in government and continuing its use in psychotherapy. It seems to me that, although her prediction has been accurate with regard to increased seeking for personal growth and self-knowledge, we have not used this overall knowledge to a very great extent in the larger society. In her final chapter, Faraday goes "Beyond The Third State," (humanistic psychology) and into dreams of creative inspiration, "lucid" dreaming, and transcendental dreams. Perhaps this will be the area in which we finally "move beyond" and really allow ourselves to use the "dream power" of which Faraday speaks.

Reference and Suggested Reading:

Faraday, Ann, *Dream Power.* New York: McCann & Geoghegan, 1972.

Faraday, Ann and Wren-Lewis, John, "The Selling of the Senoi," www.sawka.com, an account of Faraday's anthropological studies with the Senoi tribe of Malaysia and her quarrel with the work reported by Kilton Stewart. Published in "Lucidity Newsletter" 1991.

Faraday, Ann, "An Account of 'Realization of Emptiness,'" www.geocities.com, Adapted extracts from an article entitled "Towards a No-Self Psychology" in the Australian magazine, Consciousness, June 1993.

Chapter Fourteen

SURVEY YOURSELF
& OTHERS:
Type & Frequency of Dreams

HAVE YOU EVER DREAMED OF:
Falling
Arriving too late
Failing an examination

HAVE YOU EVER HAD:
A dream in color
A dream that happened
A dream about your childhood
A dream about an animal

DO YOU HAVE:
A recurring dream

DO YOU:
Remember your dreams on a
frequent basis
Tell your dreams to someone else

Now develop findings and write about what you have learned about yourself and others.

Chapter Fifteen

PSYCHIC PHENOMENA & DREAMS OF FORETELLING

"Without going outside,
you may know the whole world.
Without looking through the window,
You may see the ways of heaven.
Tao Te Ching, Lao Tsu, (6th Century B.C.)

Did you ever have a dream that happened? This kind of dream is called a "pre-cognitive dream," and many people do have them, perhaps as many as half of the people I have questioned. Most of these dreams are of events that later happen in the life of the dreamer. A small percentage of these people have dreams that predict happenings in the "larger society," such as plane crashes or the death of a public figure. An even smaller percentage have written down and dated these "larger society" dreams and/or discussed them ahead of time with another person. When you keep a dream journal, you may be surprised to find that a good number of your dreams do happen.

At one time in my life, I had a series of pre-cognitive dreams in which the events actually happened fairly soon after the occurrence of the dream. I believe these dreams were "sent" to me simply to confirm that such events are possible. The most impressive was a dream where I took a crystal heart to someone I knew, who worked in a downtown shop. In my dream, I gave him the heart, and he kissed me. Did I have a choice? Could I stay home, never deliver the heart and never collect the kiss? I don't know. I followed the dream, and went to town. I gave the heart to my friend, and he kissed me. I received a precious moment with a lovely person I cared about very much. My own heart "went out to him," for he had just recently lost his little girl to death. I gave him the crystal heart to help heal his own heart. How could I dream ahead of time of someone else's actions? I don't think anyone knows the answer to this question, certainly I do not.

"Psychic phenomena" in dreams and in waking life have to do with information that comes to us from internal or external sources of which we are not ordinarily aware, i.e., extra-sensory perception. There are numerous types of psychic phenomena that might be noticed in dreams. You might have a "dream of foretelling" or a dream that explains events from the past that were previously unknown to you. Sometimes a "dream of foretelling" gives us a chance to change our behavior to avoid the outcome in the dream. For example, if you dream of a plane crash and decide to cancel your flight and the plane crashes without you, then you have a pretty vivid demonstration that this is not all "just nonsense!" Someone who has died may appear to you in a dream in such a way that it is more than "dreaming about" the person. Rather, you may feel clearly that the person is communicating with you from the "other side." You may have what you feel is a "past life" dream. Much of our interpretation of dreams of psychic phenomena will depend upon our own belief system regarding life after death, reincarnation, and other spiritual beliefs. (Holzer, 1973)

In their 10 year long research regarding psychic phenomena in dreams, Montague Ullman, M.D., a psychiatrist and psychoanalyst and Stanley Krippner, Ph.D., a psychologist, with Alan Vaughn a psychic and writer, conducted extensive experiments with "dream telepathy" at the Dream Laboratory of Maimondes Medical Center in Brooklyn, New York. They utilized discoveries regarding REM sleep and had their subjects sleep while being monitored with EEG apparatus. As the sleepers (the receivers) experienced REM states, other participants (the senders) viewed reproductions of selected art work and attempted to "send" the images to the sleeping "receiver." Elaborate safeguards were developed so that the receiver had no knowledge of the image to be sent, nor did the sender until he or she opened a sealed envelope. The sender and receiver were separated by several rooms and locked doors. The sleeping receiver was awakened after each REM period to recount dream content. In addition, after awakening in the morning, the sleepers were given an opportunity to discuss their dreams. Only then were the sleepers allowed to see the images that had been "sent." The dream symbols that were reported were rated for correspondence to the image by a panel and by the dreamer on the basis of "hits" corresponding to the image. The greatest number of hits were recorded after sending a striking image of Christ being taken from the cross, "The Descent from the Cross," by Max Beckmann. Results that were "far beyond chance" were documented in several different parts of the study. Ullman and Krippner are great students and teachers of dreams and dreaming and are still working in the field today.

Their student, Robert Van deCastle, Ph.D., was a participant in the dream telepathy study. Like other sleepers in the study, he slept and dreamed and reported for eight nights over a three month period. Van deCastle was dubbed the "prince of percipients" by Ullman and Krippner for his ability to report the most accurate dream symbols. Van deCastle, who made an extensive study of dreams in many cultures, has recently published an encyclopedic volume titled *Our Dreaming Mind* (1994), wherein he includes a chapter titled "Paranormal Dreams." In that chapter, he discusses the Maimondes experiments as well as his own work, using a "Dream Helper Ceremony" he developed with Henry Reed. In the Dream Helper Ceremony approach, the goal is to "dream collectively about a target person's problem and to help that person find a solution to the problem." Van deCastle found this approach inspiring and helpful to a large percentage of participants, and concludes: "If the time ever comes when we all agree to use the formidable power of our dreaming mind as dream helpers for each other, we will witness a positive change in planetary consciousness greater than the negative change in planetary consciousness following the dropping of the first atomic bomb." (p. 438)

Sigmund Freud was interested in psychic phenomena, but he had a tendency to discount psychic events. His skepticism was one of the breaking points between himself and Carl Jung. Jung was a mystic and a visionary who, in his autobiography, detailed mystical and psychic events occurring since his childhood. Jung experienced psychic phenomena, dreams of foretelling, and visits from the dead. Many of these experiences are recounted in his autobiography, which he called *"Memories, Dreams, Reflections."*

A few years before his death, Sigmund Freud, the great skeptic, said in an interview with Hungarian writer Tabori: "The transference of thoughts, the possibility of sensing the past or the future cannot be merely accidental. Some people say,…that in my old age I have become credulous. No…I don't think so. Merely—all my life I have learned to accept new facts, humbly, readily." (Dream Telepathy, p.28)

My own impression regarding psychic phenomena in dreams and in general is that this is part of each of us learning to trust ourselves. Over time, I have developed a sense about my dreams—this is an anxiety dream, this one has to do with a past life, here is a dream where I avoid working with the symbols in the gestalt way, here is a dream that tells me the future. This dream will happen. These feelings and intuitions are part of the deep mysteries of my soul. I recommend that we value these experiences and give them our full attention as well as our thanks to dreams that come to us with inspiration and truth.

References:

Holzer, Hans, *The Psychic Side of Dreams.* NY: Doubleday, 1973.

Targ, Russell, Ph.D. & Putoff, Harold, Ph.D., *Mind-Reach. Scientists Look at Psychic Ability.* New York: Delacorte Press, 1977.

Ullman, Montague, M.D., Krippner, Stanley, M.D., Vaughan, Alan, *Dream Telepathy. Experiments in Nocturnal ESP.* Baltimore, Md: Penguin Books, 1974.

Van deCastle, Robert, *Our Dreaming Mind.* New York: Ballantine Books/Random House, 1994.

The Descent from the Cross by Max Beckmann, 1917.
This is the image that was most readily transmitted to the dreamer in the
dream telepathy experiments of Ullman, Krıppner & Vaughn.
© 2005 Artists Rights Society (ARS), New York/VG Bild-Kunst, Bonn.

Chapter Sixteen

SURVEY YOURSELF & OTHERS: Psychic Phenomena

(1) Have you ever had a "dream of foretelling?" i.e., you dreamed of something that then happened?

(2) Have you ever learned something in a dream that you hadn't known or noticed in waking life?

(3) Have you ever had a "dream of foretelling" about something that then happened in the "larger society," i.e., flood, death of a well known person, etc.?

(4) Have you ever dreamed the same dream at the same time as another person?

(5) Have you ever solved a problem or had a "creative inspiration" in a dream?

(6) Have you ever taken part in a controlled experiment to transmit material into the dream of another person?

Now develop findings and write about what you have learned about yourself and others.

Chapter Seventeen

CARL JUNG: THE COLLECTIVE UNCONSCIOUS & THE ARCHETYPES OF THE HUMAN PERSONALITY

Carl Jung: A mystic who experienced psychic
phenomena and dreams of foretelling.

"My life is a story of the self-realization of the unconscious".
C.G. Jung, 1961

Carl Jung was born in 1876 and died in 1961. Jung was a student of Freud, but he
differed with Freud on personal issues as well as Freud's theory of wish fulfillment
and what he called Freud's "exclusive sexualistic conception" of dream symbols.

For Freud, dreams are retrospective, concerned with past unresolved infantile conflicts and instinctual needs. For Jung, dreams could deal with the present and even future plans, imaginings, hopes, and dreams.

Jung believed that in addition to our personal unconscious mind, there is also a "collective unconscious," the repository for universal symbols, which transcend time and space. He called these universal symbols "archetypes," great symbols that appear in many or even all cultures; for example, male and female, birth, death and rebirth, and such aspects of personality as "the child," "the wise person," and "the trickster," which can be found in each one of us.

Many of these archetypes appear as polarities, or opposites, and Jung's work sought to move the person to integration of personality, which he called "individuation." One easily recognizable archetype is the persona and the shadow, the persona being that part of ourselves that we admire and readily show to others. Its polarity, the shadow, represents those parts of ourselves we dislike and conceal. Jung pointed out how we can recognize our persona and our shadow in our dreams and use these symbols to accept our whole self.

Jung was a great student of Eastern philosophy and integrated these studies into his work. The yin/yang symbol is an Oriental symbol that illustrates the male/female polarity and is also a Mandala, or "magic circle." The Yin/Yang symbol is familiar now in our culture and illustrates both polarity and integration.

Yin Yang

Jung also developed personality theories about the introverted or extroverted person and the four functions of the personality, which he designated as thinking, feeling, judging, and perceiving. This aspect of his work has been adapted into "personality tests" such as the "Briggs-Myers Personality Type Indicator."

Jung was a mystic who experienced his own dreams of foretelling and other psychic phenomena. His most readable book is his autobiography, *Memories, Dreams, Reflections,* first published in 1961, the year of his death.

Reference:

Jung, C.G., *Memories, Dreams, Reflections.* New York: Random house, 1961.

Sugestions for Future Reading:

Fincher, Suzanne F., *Creating Mandalas for Insight, Healing and Self Expression.*

Boston, Mass: Shambhala Publications, Inc., 1991.

VonFranz, Marie Louise, *Time, Rhythm and Repose.* New York: Thames and Hudson, 1978.

Wilhelm, Richard and Jung, C.G., *The Secret of the Golden Flower: A Chinese Book of Life.* New York: Harcourt, Brace & World, Inc., 1962.

Chapter Eighteen

DREAMS, ANIMALS & THE AFTERLIFE

"Into the great wide open
Under them skies of blue
Out in the great wide open
A rebel without a clue."
Tom Petty (1991)

Most of what I have seen clearly about the afterlife has come to me in dreams and visions. Now that I am a bit older, I do not look forward to the clarity of the perceptions and inspirations that, in the past, have moved me to poetry and written remembrances, for it means that another dear one has left her or his physical body and moved beyond, into the "afterlife," or "other world," as it was called by the ancient Celts. Now I can no longer touch that precious body, exchange a kiss, a hug, a few words in person or even a phone call, and must depend on what visions and dreams are allowed to me to contact loved ones who are no longer present in their physical body.

What I will say of the dear human departed is that when I dream of them, they are dancing, and they are young again and lovely, and they speak to me with consolation.

We share our lives with our companion animals. Our bonds are so deep that, when they die, our grieving sometimes takes us into our first or deeper understanding of the life hereafter. In my experience, animals and people come into our dreams after death to bring us messages about our present day lives and to console us because we miss them so much. It seems to me that we either "dream about" someone, that someone "comes into" a dream spontaneously or that we may also "invite them" into our dreams.

When inviting the dead into our dreams, we can speak to the animal or person before going to sleep, asking them to come. We can create a before bed ritual with a candle and beautiful objects, perhaps something that belonged to the loved one.

We can bless the space, invite the spirit, and create the time to receive the loved one. We can use special music and relaxing herbs, like lavender, or scented leaves, like roses, to open our unconscious minds to an awareness of our loved one who has died. All of these processes can be used for animals or for humans, and it is well to write about our experiences as soon as we wake in the morning.

If you want to dream about someone who has died and it doesn't happen, then you can consult with a "medium." Mediums are very sensitive people who can assist you in contacting those who are in that other world or afterlife. You can, of course, create your own communications, using a dialogue with the person or animal who has died, visualizing her or him as present...and then the communication is really happening and, for just a moment, you are together again, for real!

It is the animals who have showed me the color of heaven, the green, green grass and trees, and the vibrant color of the oranges hanging on the trees. The night following his death, my dear kitty, Michael, came to me in a dream wearing a crisp black and white tuxedo to welcome me to this beautiful vision of heaven. My dear dog, Scarlett, also came to me in a dream, where I see her running on the beach, then disappearing behind the dunes, where I know for sure she is waiting for me to come and play again.

When we begin to talk with animals and communicate with the dead, we are indeed "out in the great wide open." Our clues to understanding these experiences are our dreams and our trust in our own experience. It is my belief that it is these experiences "on the edge" that challenge our creativity and lead us to our highest potential. As I move into the new century I go toward my love of animals, to learn to speak more fully with them, to use all my skills to heal them, to learn through them to truly speak of peace.

Reference:

Petty, T., and Lynne, J., Album "Into The Great Wide Open," Song "Into The Great Wide Open," 1991

Scarlett in her last Winter, 1997, Washoe Valley, NV.

Many animals look into the "great beyond" as they prepare to leave this lifetime.

Sunshine in her last Fall, 2004, Gainesville, FL.

This chapter is dedicated to all the lovely animals who have passed through my life, leaving behind them only love.

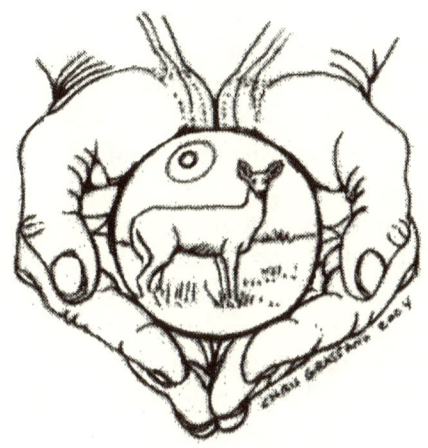

Oh, Deer!
Used by permission of the artist, Chris Grassano, 2004

Chapter Nineteen

OH, DEER! A DREAM OF COOPERATIVE HEALING

Tuesday, 1:00 PM. As I get ready to go out to do my errands. I glance out the window and see something unusual behind a bush. Oh, it's a deer's little nubbin of a tail! Nothing too unusual about that, for although I live in a neighborhood surrounded by houses, my yard is full of ivy, a circle of small trees low to the ground, and pretty green weeds. It is not unusual for the deer to stop by, for the area in front of my house is quite safe; however, I do worry about them when they stay too late in the day and have to brave traffic on their way home to the nearby canyon—so this time of day is unusual and somewhat dangerous for a deer visit.

As I watch her grazing around the trees, I realize that one foot or leg is injured. She can stand and walk but cannot put her weight on her left hind leg. I decide to be very quiet and wait until she leaves. I begin to send her Reiki with Rescue

Remedy on my hands, I visualize holding her foot, massaging her hind quarters and leg with Arnica and Calendula, and I pray to the Holy Mother to heal her. Eventually, I abandon my errands and stay quietly in my house, communicating to the deer to rest quietly and safely in my yard. Late in the afternoon, I leave messages for my landlady and her sister that an injured deer is in the yard, please do not startle her or chase her away.

Finally, it is dark. I communicate to the deer to continue to wait until all traffic has cleared. The landlady's sister comes banging on my door, wanting to approach the deer. She cannot hear me and in order to stop her, I yell at her to leave the deer alone, making a substantial amount of noise of my own and causing me to feel badly afterwards and to apologize. But the deer does not bolt and, late in the evening, she is still there. I call several friends and ask them to send Reiki, prayers, and healing to the deer.

In the morning, the deer is gone. At noon my friend calls me to tell me her dream: "A baby deer is with her mother, she has a bandage on her left rear ankle." I cry tears of relief. The deer is safe with her mom. Two days later, early in the morning, I open my front door to see the deer sitting very close, just down the path from my front porch. She stands up and very deliberately stretches her left hind leg, gently bringing her foot to the ground. She stands down on all four legs, slightly favoring the injured leg. Two days later, she comes again, showing me nearly full weight-bearing on the injured leg. I give thanks and know that love and healing do survive in the Universe, and "I get by," as the Beatles said, "with a little help from my friends."

Chapter Twenty

THE TIMELESS DREAM & MY GRANDMOTHER'S PANTRY

The Dream of April 11, 1976:
"Vincent is there, but I don't see him. The author of the
Rank book lives there. He looks like Rank. He takes
me downstairs to a room. I can see in the door. The
walls are lined with cubbyholes full of drugs.
The drugs look like different kinds of grains and corn.
A man is in the room. He looks like 'the lifeguard.'
I feel the presence of 'the picture.' I am frightened."

This is one of the first dreams I ever recorded in a dream journal. I had met
Vincent O'Connell in the Fall of 1975 and began to study gestalt therapy under
his supervision. The location of the dream is his house in my hometown,
Daytona Beach, Florida. I remembered the dream from time to time, reliving
those years, rich and full with study and learning, but I never really "worked" on
the dream, which I now know to be one of the greatest gifts ever received from
my inner self.

January 1999, Carmel, California:
I stand in my kitchen in Carmel, 23 years later and 3000 miles away from the
dream, looking at my kitchen shelves, at the jars of grains and beans, herbs and
remedies. Suddenly I remember the Timeless Dream and I realize I have at long
last, through time and space, arrived at the place of the dream.

I am struck immediately and very strongly that the dream was precognitive,
manifesting now after such a long period of time. Twenty-three years ago, I did
not base my diet on grains and beans, and my foods were not my medicines, as
they are now. I had not become—or even thought of becoming—an herbalist,

nor did I use herbal remedies. Now, this lifestyle intertwines with the wholeness of my life and livelihood.

As I continue to face my kitchen stores, I begin to remember my grandmother's pantry. The look of the shelves, so like mine, brings vivid remembrance of the guava jelly, fig preserves, or perhaps cookies for a children's tea party, always brought forth with a smile and her soft Southern voice saying, "Would you like this, Hon?" Abundance dwelt in that pantry, treats and indulgences for a little girl.

On the shadow side of the pantry, I remember the separate dishes kept for the "colored girl," and the bell that was used to summon this dignified and kindly woman from the kitchen to serve at family dinners. My embarrassment was deep and my puzzlement was great that my beloved grandparents could behave so wrongly to devalue another person. Even when I was very young, I knew that, even though she was working for our family, she could certainly eat from our dishes. The summons of a ringing bell felt wrong to me. I knew that, somehow, these actions were demeaning to this person and that it was happening simply because her skin was darker than ours. From that time on, I have searched for answers about equality and social justice.

The Timeless Dream moved me, in the present day, to struggle with my own prejudices, to again forgive myself, and my family, to seek the roots of ignorance and unknowing hatred and to face the need to continue with the work of love.

Coming from the past to the relevance of the dream in the here-and-now, I created many dialogues with the creatures of the dream. The "lifeguard," for example, turned around with a grin and identified himself as a trickster, luring me ever deeper into my own unconscious mind. I spent some fruitful time pondering, becoming aware of, and owning up to the ways I trick myself, my denials, the ways I get what I want, the things I resist, and how I create my scenarios of success and failure.

The Timeless Dream even moved me toward the Year 2000 and questions about stocking up in case of communication and delivery failures or the like. In my family, the pantry was kept stocked in case of emergency, for hurricane season, or when unexpected company came to visit. If a hurricane was on the way, we would fill the bathtub with extra water and get out the Sterno stove for cooking. Then, independent of the elements, we'd settle into home until the storm passed. Company at any time could be welcomed and fed with food put by for such occasions. The dream reminds me of the pleasure of "simple abundance," the extra can of tomatoes, treats for unexpected guests, and the good feeling that comes from "being prepared" and having enough to share, as well as enough for myself

The final gift of the Timeless Dream came just today, as I sat to do this writing. I looked at the wholeness of the dream, at the "mandala of the pantry," I had created and, suddenly, I put myself "in the picture," the one big symbol I could not approach for all these years. I looked into the picture frame and saw my own reflection there. I said to myself, "Hello, Elizabeth." My self replied, "Hello, Elizabeth." At that moment, I left my fear behind and found myself whole.

Elizabeth Howard: "I found myself whole."

CONCLUSION

Tuesday, October 21, 2003. After of almost two weeks of "writer's block," I have finished the book. Even though I know there will be another editorial review, more polishing, a bit more research just to be sure, the actual writing down of ideas is done. I can't figure out what to do to celebrate and I feel that I have a lot of time to spare. I haven't realized how absorbed I have been in the writing. I now have that familiar feeling that I don't want to finish, I'm valuing what seemed like stress, anxiety, hard work and worry.

As a reward, I received a beautiful dream. I wake in the night realizing that I am dreaming of the reason I came into this lifetime. "They" are talking and talking and explaining to me. When I wake in the morning, I have forgotten the words, the directions and the explanations. What is left, blazing in vivid colors before my eyes, is one word:

Peace

It is written in beautiful script and surrounded by beautiful, full blown roses, deep pink, with silver edges.

This is the beauty I wait for, this is why I love to dream.

ABOUT THE AUTHOR

Elizabeth Howard has her M.A. and certification in Gestalt Therapy. She has worked as a counselor and educator for 30 years. Her specialty is dreamwork.

Howard is a Florida native. She lives in Gainesville, Florida, where she offers holistic counseling, dreamwork and animal communication. She can be reached at holisticliz@hotmail.com.

978-0-595-37626-1
0-595-37626-6